T0314877

ANGRY

Josh Overton

ANGRY

Music and Lyrics by Josh Overton and Mair Mills

OBERON BOOKS
LONDON

WWW.OBERONBOOKS.COM

First published in 2015 by Oberon Books Ltd
521 Caledonian Road, London N7 9RH
Tel: +44 (0) 20 7607 3637 / Fax: +44 (0) 20 7607 3629
e-mail: info@oberonbooks.com
www.oberonbooks.com

A catalogue record for this book is available from the British
Library.

PB ISBN: 9781783199662
E ISBN: 9781783199679

Visit www.oberonbooks.com to read more about all our books
and to buy them. You will also find features, author interviews and
news of any author events, and you can sign up for e-newsletters
so that you're always first to hear about our new releases.

ANGRY was first performed by the Pub Corner Poets from the 21 to the 23 of October 2014 in The New Adelphi Club, Hull.

Its original cast were:

A: Ellie Jane Richards
B: Josh Overton
C: Adam Hutton
D: Jamie Ferguson
E: Tyler Mortimer
F: Mair Mills
The Bassist: Meg Humphries
Young Woman: Alix Rainsby

Producer: Tyler Mortimer
Directors: Oliver Strong and Kerala Irwin
Musical Director: Mair Mills
Production Manager: Siana-Mae Heppell-Secker
Stage Manager: Alix Rainsby
Costume Designer: Adam Hutton
Technical Manager: Jamie Ferguson
Front of House Manager: Constance Lane

Thanks:

This play could never have existed without the kindness and patience of Paul Jackson, owner of the spit and sawdust, kickass corner of the world we call home: The New Adelphi Club and the never-ending help in the form of coffee and publicity from the infinitely charming Maddie Rose, owner of The English Muse. Thanks also to David Byrne of The New Diorama Theatre for constantly pushing us to do better and to Rob Salmon of the New Wolsey Theatre for teaching me everything I know and giving us lovely money.

I dedicate this play to Tyler Mortimer, thank you for your constant inspiration, your unending passion for my writing and for doing far more work than I had any right to expect you to do.

Characters

A – The Groupie

B – The Frontman

C – The Writer

D – The Drummer

E – The Comedian

F – The Shy One

WHERE?
[The theatre you are watching this in]

WHEN?
[The time you are watching it at]

WHAT?
[A Stage]

[There is nothing but what the band needs on stage, we see [A] [B] [D] [E] and [F] in various states of undress and with various instruments strapped to them, [C] should be well dressed and, whatever his age, should have an older demeanour than the others] [Next to them a small table for drinks, throughout the play the cast will smoke and drink as little or as much as they feel the need to. Until the end the character of [B] will be the only one smoking "Joints", and he should smoke them a lot. Too much in fact.]

[Pages of the script litter the stage]

[Several mics are set far in front of them and a young woman [A], is stood in front of one of them. All of them take in the audience as they take their seats, perhaps they improvise songs or interact with them until the piece is ready to begin]

[[A] steps up to the mic when she is satisfied that her audience have settled and begins the play]

[The Play is called 'Angry.']

[The Play is a mess]

[She loves the Play as do the others]

#1 – In which we meet our heroes and learn about their play.

A: 'Fuck'

Is the first word of this play

The last word is 'me'

But we'll get to that later.

'Fuck'

>Sound it out with me,

>>Fuuuuuuuuuuuuuuck.

It's okay, I'm not your mum,
I'm not some kind of fucking cunt
fuck you for swearing parent
or teacher,
too tired to reach you
writing you off for bein' who you wanna be

try it out

FUUUUUUUCK.

[She seems pleased if her audience react]

A: Interesting isn't it? I hope you find me interesting,
I want you to find me interesting.
That's why you're here,
At least,
Some, of why,

You're here.

[She pauses for a moment as if unsure of herself, before settling down and continuing]

A: There's gonna be a lot of fucks by the way,

like

a loooot of fucking fucks,

so many fucking fucks in fucking fact that we thought we'd make a game of it. So, *[she surveys the audience, maybe she tosses a beer to one or two of them as she produces a set of instruction cards as if from a board game and begins to read]*

#1 Every time we drop a swear out of no where take a drink

ya cunts

#2 Every time one of us forgets our lines take a drink, partly for the game

mostly to fill the awkward pause.

Uhhhh

#3 Every time you crane your neck to get a better look at my tits. Drink

That's for boys and girls I have a very nice bra ladies and you may want to ask where I got it after the show.

[if the theatre doesn't have an alcohol license]
Oh by the way

This place doesn't have a liquor license so if someone who looks suspiciously like an usher asks, these bottles are not alcohol free ones that we've poured out and replaced with real booze that doesn't taste like witch's piss.

A: *[Addressing a woman in the audience]* What's your name sweetheart?
[No matter the woman's response she replies:] Huh, no way, that's my name.

I'll bet you hate your parents too huh darling?

[NOTE: For the rest of the play [A] will be referred to by the cast as the woman's name that she has adopted, this will be represented in the script with an [A], this also applies to the rest of the cast once they've taken their names.]

A: Let me tell you why you're here,

Let me fill you in as it were.

In a good way

Not a dirty way

Although I will if you're free after sweetheart, I'll take you out back and make sweet love with you on the
soft
moonlight reflecting
piss-stained streets of *[wherever the gig is]*

Let me tell you why we wrote this,

Why

This was

Built.

All of the words are ours.

And

Most of the music is ours

And most of

Most of the stories are

Ours

Everything we say has been thought by someone

At some point.

Some of it was written here *[She produces a book with 'The Little Book of Angry Thoughts' scribbled on the cover, she tosses this book into the audience for them to look at] [NOTE: The book should consist mostly of drawings both aggressive and funny but other than that its contents are a decision to be made by the cast]*

A: But most of it came from in our heads.

Oh and *[returning to her namesake audience member]* of course yours, I shan't be forgetting you *[She uses her name]*

We wrote this play thinking of you *[She uses her name]*

[beat]

I didn't mean it by the way *[She uses her name]*

I don't hate my parents *[She uses her name]*

Or yours *[She uses her name]*

I'm sure they're lovely *[She uses her name]*

You seem

Real

Nice.

[The guitar riff from the beginning returns interrupting what has become a moment of distraction, seamlessly she returns to the script building energy with the music]

A: This play is called 'Angry.'

And this play is a mess.

Messy in a 'fuck you
mum I'll clean my room
when you stop sucking off
the neighbour's son'

Kinda Way.
Why 'Angry.'?

Cuz if we'd called it Happy

Or Breakfast at fucking Tiffany's

You'd have left quite disappointed tonight wouldn't you.

This play is like riding a bike down a set of stairs
You're shitting yourself, hoping it'll go right and you're
parents'd be very upset if they knew what you were doing
but when you get to the bottom you may well feel like
you've actually experienced something.

> This play is called Angry.
> Because it thrives on it.

If it weren't so Angry there'd be no words for it

If it weren't so Angry there'd be no music to it

If it weren't so Angry there'd be no

Whoever you think I am.
Token slut? Groupie? Felate you fifty times a day for a
fiver? Somebody's daughter? *[shrug]*

Whatever it is you know I look far too good in a bra and
shorts to cut from the show.

[She mock felates the mic as [B] begins to drive the music]

My name is [A],

We are ANGRY. And for one night only

SO ARE YOU.

This is OUR play

This is OUR night.

And this night is about US.

YOU ME WE US

This play is not about binge drinking
Or anonymous sex
This play is not about drug overdoses
Or Smoking Sixteen CigaretteS a day
This play is not about fights in the street
A and E visits or
Brothers in prison

This Play is not about lying to your parents
Or the Police
It's not about riots
It's not about violence
or suicide

But it could have been
Easily.

A: This play is called Angry. And the first word of this play is
'FUCK'

SONG #1 FUCK.

I sold my soul for a drinking jar
Paid out eight hours of my life to make a wage
I live five feet from the nearest bar
But that's more than I can handle at this stage

FUCK AM I ANGRY

This play is not about celebration,
rioting, rewriting history or
lying
to parents, police or pastors
This play is not about selling tickets
As musicians or actors
This play is not about Confusion

or Seclusion or refusing
To find
a sort of suicide of the mind
So this play is not about growing up.
It is not about sexual violence
Screaming til you throw up
A mother's silence
A Father's absence
A daughter's whinings,
Tantalising Two timings
tripling in twenty years

This play is not about a lack of finance
Or "spiritual guidance"
buyer's remorse and childhood fears

Or our reliance
on drugs and dance music.
Or looking at the fucked up state of the world and saying
"Who did it?"
It's about grabbing you by the shirt

Slapping you like a little bitch
And saying "Who didn't?"

FUCK AM I ANGRY

[After the song [A] returns to the mic with a sheet of paper. On it is a speech – introducing the next scene – in the shape of a middle finger, she reads it as if it has just been thrust into her hands by [B], because it has.]

SCENE 1

IN WHICH WE

HEAR   THE

TALE   OF 1

TINY   BOY

WHO   PLAY

S BA   SS AN

D SMOKES   50 A DAY,

WHI   SK   Y I   N THE

JAR   IS   HIS   FA VOUR

ITE SO NG   AS   IT   MA   KES

HI   M H   AP   PY IN

WA   YS   HE

CA   N'T   QUITE

UN   DERS   STAN

D.   HE'S

GO   NNA

TALK   SOME

TRU   THS

TO   Y'ALL

AND   PLAY

SOM   E SW

EEEEEETSONGSTOILLUSRATEHIS
POINT. IN FACT HE WROTE THIS I-
NTRO AND... OH, DO I HAVE TO?
[HERE THE ACTORS ARE TO PRE-
TEND THAT [B] HAS WRITTEN A
SERIES OF CRUDE JOKES ABOUT
WHATEVER FLAVOR OF HUMAN
[A] IS. SHEEP JOKES ABOUT THE
WELSH, HEROIN ABOUT THE SC-
OTCH, ETC. SHE READS THEM]

[NOTE. It is imperative that the cast as a whole get drunk in a rehearsal and decide how best to make fun of the actress playing [A] and wherever it is she comes from]

[Once the boys and [F] have shouted her into "reading" out the jokes [A] pins the previous page to the front of the mic stand, steps back and fixes herself a drink/rolls a cigarette and [B] – the front man – steps up to the mic in her place.]

#2 – In which we explore the philosophical merits of kicking children, insulting cultists and watching television

B: Alright out there? Lot of boring motherfuckers in tonight, s'always good for a laugh.

Right, you've probably figured out the pattern of things already, half-naked person stands in front of microphone talks in an overly teen-in-your-face manner insults someone in the audience and then they play a bit of music.

Lather rinse repeat.

Am I riiiiiight?

But as you'll probably see I have a tendency to fall apart after a while of doing one thing for too long so I'll try be quick – this bit used to be twice as long but we cut it down 'cause I kept getting distracted

So

Hello. I Hope you are

Enjoying yourselves.

Right.

Oh I forgot the, uh. ha.

[He takes the instruction cards and reads them out again word for word]

#1 Every time we drop a swear out of nowhere take a drink

ya cunts

**#2 Every time one of us forgets our lines take a
drink,**
partly for the game
      mostly to fill the awkward pause.

**#3 Every time you crane your neck to get a better
look at my tits.**

Don't drink, you've already had way too much.

[beat]

Yeah the speech, cool, right.

Look I'm not a psycho right...

A: *[from somewhere behind]* Debatable!

B: FUCK

Take a drink.

Right.

I'm not a psycho right, but sometimes I see like, a little
kid in the street or wherever and I just wanna kick it, like
a football, over the trees and into the sun. I don't hate
kids or anything, they don't get on my tits like, I just have
that urge. You know what I mean, that uuuuurge. To do
the absolute worst thing you can think of in any given
situation. Like, alright, sometimes I walk past one of them
red post box things in the street yeah? and all I can think is
"post your wallet, go on man it'll be such an effort after but
you totally wanna do it."

You feel it like a...pulling, in this moment, you get to hold
your future entirely in your own hands, you get to be in
charge for one tiny precious little second and just for once
you get to decide the direction of your shitty little
squitty little

life. And isn't it just fucking telling that the only way you can find that level of control is to intentionally piss away all your good feelings for the day?
ALRIGH'
When I throw a brick through an old lady's front window I feel like a proper cunt, right? An' when I hunt down the biggest brick shithouse in a club and call him a faggot I'm not exactly fucking rewarded for it am I? But I really just

Can't

Help myself.

When you stand and look over the edge of a bridge and it's high up enough to kill you or whatever and the wind's all blowing at you, you feel that spray on your face, taste the salt like, it's the gravity, you feel it
pulling at you, willing you
                    needing you. To just do one stupid thing
once.

[BEAT]

[Singling out a bloke] What's your name pal? *[Again, no matter the man's response he replies:]* Huh, no way. That's what they called me without asking my permission first...

[NOTE: same as before]

B: I wrote that last song, you enjoy it? *[He uses the man's name]* You look like you enjoyed it.

Well I like it.

Why aren't other people consistent *[uses the man's name]*? I know I'm not the only one who thinks that.

All the time. People change their minds. At the drop of a hat like,

One minute they love your show then they go right off it
when the scrawny fuck starts talking to them *[He chuckles
sardonically and begins to get more aggressive]*

B: You know, [B] when you watch the telly like a sitcom or
whatever and you see these fucking paragons of social
interaction these people who're all so fucking charismatic
and pretty and,
you ever wonder what it's like for the shitheads
who aren't as funny
or as gorgeous
as you
or me
who just sit in the corners making everyone uncomfortable,
silently being a prick with a real fucking face on 'em?

You reckon it's easier or harder to be yourself if nobody
cares about you?
You know what I reckon?
I reckon it doesn't fuckin' matter. I reckon shag all'd
change if you and me figured it all out right here and now.

What about you *[B]* you cool? Reckon' people like you? Is
that cause you're consistent?

I'm consistent, consistently consistent. I like to think I am,
at least when I hang my head off the side of a bridge and
feel that soft oh so sexy little pull,
    the need to just
        let
            go
I don't, I never have and I fucking won't.

*[For a moment, he pauses. Distracted by various thoughts
eventually, [C] throws something at him to get his attention and
he jumps back on track.]*

B: Why you paid to come here. Scene 1: I am the best
motherfucking frontman you have ever met, *[beat]* I mean,
I'm not, I'm just arrogant. I've been doing this for... *[he
motions to a new audience member]* how long have I been

doing this sir/mam? _____ Days, weeks months, years,
cool. I've been doing this for _____[Days, weeks, months,
years], and I'm the best fucking frontman you have ever
seen,
at the age of sixteen I used to snort coKe and fucK
hooKers in dreams
and all I ever wanted to do was to never have to do anything.

At home, you'd see me dragging school book bags
through front doors kicked in to the tune of angry mother
screaming

D+A: *[screeching like aliens]* WERE YOU BORN IN A BARN!

A+D+B+E: FUCK OFF MUM!

B: Next upstairs

Bag goes

Clunk
    On each
        step

B: There are holes in my sister's door from where I've kicked
it in, in one of my now family famous angry rages
to her credit she's stuck a poster print out of Jack Nicholson
screaming

D: *[Hitting drums like an axe to a door]* Heeeeere's Johnny!

B: In one of the bigger gaps so it looks like Stanley Kubrick
has told him to murder you with an axe as you walk by.
Every day after school I'd wedge my coat under the
bottom of my bedroom door
to mask the smell
                and light a joint,

listen to Hendrix.
Sometimes I'd have a wank.
And I'm not ashamed of that.
Sometimes I'd have a wank,
    get ash all piling up in my pants

and not notice till I went for a piss and saw my cock had turned grey.

[He checks his pants]

After some time of puberty fuelled whiney teen drug smokey

A: FUCK OFF MUM

B: cum

E: FUU OOOF DAAAA

B: Cum

D: Fuck off Mr. Math Teacher Cunt

B: Cum

D+E+A: Fuck off Great aunt Bertha

B: Cum, heh *[A, B, D and E chuckle, C is expressionless]*

B: After more than some time of that Some old fuck from next door comes knocking for a fucking grumble about the smoke or the smell or the arrangement of the flowers out front or how no one respects him for fighting in the war and then doing nothing worthwhile with his life after, and the house is totally empty except for yours truly so, I'm high as balls like packing my grey cock away and answering the door to this bloke who's talking some shit about the council and hedges being too big or whatever and all I'm thinking is:

B: Go the fuck away
Go the fuck away
Go the fuck away
Go the fuck away
Go the fuck away
Go the fuck away
Go the fuck away
Go the fuck away
Go the fuck away
Go the fuck away
[And Breeeaaath.]
Go the fuck away
Go the fuck away
Go the fuck away
Go the fuck away
Go the fuck away
Go the fuck away
Go the fuck away
Go the fuck away
GO THE FUCK AWAY
GO THE FUCK AWAY
GO THE FUCK AWAY
GO THE FUCK AWAY
GO THE FUCK AWAY
GO THE FUCK AWAY
GO THE FUCK AWAY
GO THE FUCK AWAY
GO THE FUCK AWAY
GO THE FUCK AWAY
GO THE FUCK AWAY
GO THE FUCK AWAY

D: *[Affecting an elderly voice]*
You see young man, I'm
an extremely boring old
cunt with nothing better
to do than remind you of
your own mortality and
talk about spics and wogs
and how IN MY DAY
no one was a queer like
today. It's PC gone mad
these days I'll be voting
UKIP the hippies hate
this country they should
all get a haircut and join
the army like I pretend
I did but have you seen
my teeth? Where's my
hair, I've misplaced my
wife The government is
spying on my legs do you
want a WERTHER'S
ORIGINAL? I WEAR
SOCK SUSPENDERS
AND PLAY BOULES
ON MY DAYS
OFF WHEN I'M
NOT SMILING
CONDESCENDINGLY
FOR OVER 50's
LIFE INSURANCE
ADVERTS
WHAT'S A DVD!!!!?!?!
COUNTDOWN IS
GOOOOOD!!!!!
[breathe]

B: You...get the idea with that.

23

So after like ten years of standing and swearing behind my eyes at this crusty prick, I close the door, wired as shit, my high's gone and the fucking thoughts are back, I wanna do something stupid: Jump off bridges – brick through window stupid shit I was talking about like 2 minutes ago *[to the most un-entertained looking audience member he can find]* KEEP UP PIGFUCKER! *[a drumbeat from [D] brings him back on track] [[C] lights a match the 'pigfucker' audience member becomes the frog of the story to him in the next few moments]* So I'm bouncing off the walls thinking about setting a match to this little frog fuck I can see on the patio out back and the frog's staring back at me goading me like,

[in a Ray Winston gangster voice] 'you don't have the balls [B], do it, burn me you sissy fuck, existence is pain for a frog.'

And I'm coming round to the way of thinking that maybe I'd be doing the frog a favour by ending a lifetime of suffering with a short period of extreme fiery suffering when the doorbell goes again *[he blows the match out and eyes the pigfucker frog person as if to say 'you're safe for now']* and standing there is some empty-looking cunt in a suit with no tie and someone who must have been his daughter, maybe a couple years younger than me cute little thing, blonde but with this fucking smile like, teeth just everywhere, they both looked like they didn't know we were all slowly dying and I'm thinking:

B: Oh shit is this gonna be about...

E: [in a mad cult voice] Hello sir have you heard of JEEESSSUUUUS?

Fuck.
And this douchebag starts waxing lyrical about some hokey shit that makes no sense, like

E: DID YOU KNOW that if we ignore all evidence to the contrary and pretend that the starving Ethiopian children who die of AIDS every day in some sort of ironic 'thought they'd die of hunger' way, if we pretend they don't exist then we can see the majestic work of God in every facet of human existence and reality itself?

B: *[he picks out a woman in the audience to fixate on now]* I'm just staring at his daughter's tits like but he goes on talking without missing a beat, he's religious he doesn't want honest fucking responses does he.

E: Do you know anything of original sin young man?

B: *[still looking at tits]* I...

E: THAT'S RIGHT, when humans had just been created THAT'S RIGHT CREATED no matter what Darwin that foul homosexual paedophile birdwatching SHIT says, when we'd just been created by GUUUURD our ancestor Adam and his naked friend Eve who was made out of one of his ribs because of reasons, met a talking snake, well I say snake the BIBLE *[he manically throws a Bible at [B] who completely ignores it]* calls it a 'serpent' because that sounds fancier and GUURD uses fancy words because he's smarter than you or I brother –

B: That's creepy, don't call me brother –

E: No problem brother, they met a talking snake who told them to eat the fruit of the tree of knowledge so that they might have some tasty knowledge all to themselves and OBVIOUSLY when GUUURD found out he kicked them out of his nice garden and made them do incest with their kids to make breed the human race.

B: kay

E: And that is why brother

B: Creepy

E: we must all feel guilty all the time, for when several thousand years ago someone you don't know on the advice of a limbless reptile did something bad that you had no control over – like eating fruit – you must be prepared to accept the blame. It must be true because someone once said it was and no one would make this up am I right? Amen.

B: *[back to storytelling]* That's the general gist of what he said anyway, I don't really remember and/or give a fuck what I do remember and/or give a fuck about is by now I've caught the eye of his daughter who's looking a lot less teethy
when her dad – I assume it's her dad – isn't watching, she keeps giving me these 'sorry about this senseless prick' looks that I always do when I'm introducing him *[motions to [D]]* to people.

D: *[Totally calm]* Go fuck a landmine.

B: Cheers pal, mad love. Uuuuh where am I?

C: Page 15...Showing off. Drink.

B: Yes, good, thanks,

So I'm wanting to show off and impress this girl – I'm fucking sixteen at this point anything with even slight tit is interesting to me so I turn to look at this dude who's got that face on like 'please validate what I've said because if you don't I might start thinking for myself and realise I've been lied to all these years' and – ah *[he starts to chuckle softly]* I look him straight in the eye just like my daddy never taught me to do and say summin like

'Sir, ten minutes ago I was genuinely considering trying to set alight a frog because I couldn't quite convince myself it wasn't making fun of me, I even gave it a Ray Winston accent like, and I was in the middle of coming up with his violent but quietly dignified gangster back story when you rang my doorbell and even I think you might be a little bit mental.'

B: And so he storms off with a sort of

E: Hw urg? BLURGH Shnur glerp BRRAAARG!

B: And I got the girl's number, she was pretty and I was happy, I fucking *[a pause, he tries to sound more sincere]* I fucking cared about her, which was nice, a new feeling.

[[C] has noticed the momentary lapse on [B]'s part and begins to look annoyed]

This is where the story stops being a metaphysical wank-fest and gets a bit more relevant. See this girl introduced me, myself and Irene to proper television.
Now I was raised on the tiny screen, father mother brother sister lover teacher and everything in between but up 'til then all we had was terrestrial so some days it was watching 'neighbours', 'hollyoaks' 'eastenders' or nothing,

I chose nothing on those days cuz I'm not a vacuous cunt.

But now here's a pretty thing with money who wants to lick my face and call me sir and what do we do when old [B] junior here is all worn out? *[quickly he snaps back to the audience member whose name he has adopted]* Do you call yours that *[he uses his name]*? I'm talking about your willy.

What does one do when one is spent enough to be done with sex for a week but *[beat]* genuinely in love enough to just stay in bed and hold hands?

You watch all the television there is.

And it's fucking brilliant.

SONG #2 Slave to the Screen

Ask them the burning questions
They'll give you steaming lies
The mass education of a nation through a Dictator's eyes
We have a new King
A king with no blood to spill
But plenty of horses and men to kill

And all for the thrill of an 8 year old boy
Whose parents thought he'd be safe
Watching the box with a shapeshifting face
Never the same and all in one place
The ceaseless pace of the bold and the brave
And the men whose only objective is more
More tits more guts more gore
This little boy saw death today
Then he saw it again
Film 4 + 1 is a fucking godsend

B: Suddenly I'm seeing adverts that are like 15 minutes long, like I'm living in fucking America or something, cartoons where people get their tits out and swear and stuff that looks like it might have cost millions – more money than I'd ever see in my life, I'm fucking hooked, it was like seeing whole parts of yourself you never knew were there just up on display for you to gawk at.

Big Brother is taking over
Man no longer needs a wife
He's got every station
And every free-thinking man across the nation needs the sensation
We have a new God
Its name is Dave it has all that you crave
But are too scared to live
Too lazy to dream
Too tired to rip from its seams to spill all its beans
Read its guts like fucking tea leaves
Maybe you'll see your future
Stitched togther with sutures this young man found
On the floor of a first person shooter

B: I swear down I saw a guy shoot his own ear off on some reality show it was fucking immense. She and I would channel surf for hours and I'd learn everything that the people who should have been paying attention were too scared to tell me.

I see rockstar rappers write rhymes in rhythms reacting
with righteous indignation, rewatch on plus one for the
reiteration

Sesame street taught me alliteration.

And I was hungry for it, everything felt so wrong but made
so much sense.

Slave to the screen
Servant of the media
Second to technology
Feeding the hysteria
Mass production
Brain matter reduction
They gave us all the tools
For our self-destruction

All eyes are glazing over
They're giving you all you need
Live humiliation castigation a circus of greed on a round the
clock feed
We have a new Leader
You'll find him in every household
He sits in the place of honour
Where all behold his wonders unfold
And the people beholding behold all the violence
The rape the murder the silence
Of children who soak up the deep seated rage
Of a passionate artist whose only wish
Was fame, fame, money and fame
The power that comes with a household name
Leaving their bloody bootprints on young tender brains

B: I see angry looking beautiful for the first time in my life.
I see celebrities forced to grovel
I see people selling souls and swapping their wives
I see retards become role models

Slave to the screen
Servant of the media
Second to technology
Feeding the hysteria
Mass production
Brain matter reduction
They gave us our orders
And we followed instructions

#3- A game not quite as insensitive as the one we'll play later and the beginning of the breakdown.

[[A] returns to the mic looking a bit more relaxed than before]

A: Me again, hey *[to her audience member]* you happy? *[before she can get a reply]* Gooooooood. Okay so we're gonna have to level with you here, they said we couldn't have the venue if we didn't fill an hour long slot and we had like 3 songs and a bit of talking so I promised them we'd pad the running time and play games and take the piss a bit so you didn't feel like you'd wasted your money come the climax and it's brilliant that that sentence has both 'come' and 'climax' within two words of each other.

[She giggles. [C] coughs louder than he needs to to get her back on track and she does]

A: Right, heheh, so we took a close look at the pre-booked tickets and thought to ourselves 'what would these massive bastards enjoy, 'cause every minute that passes is like 4 pence they've given us'

And we settled on something we felt reflected the kind of audience that'd come see a bunch of semi-naked twenty-somethings shout and moan about their pretend lives –

D: Oooooh meta!

A: So bearing all that in mind we present the first of what we hope will become an annual tradition – WHO IN THE AUDIENCE LOOKS MOST LIKE THE FRONT COVER OF OUR PORN MAG!

D: *[Having leapt out of his seat and grabbing one of the magazines that [C] has stacked up before running to the mic]* IT'S LIKE A SEXY VERSION OF 'GUESS WHO'!

[Music is played by everyone as he dives into the audience and begins searching, giggling like a child but not nearly as creepily as that sounds]

A: *[in the voice of a T.V. presenter]* Today's show is brought to you by 3 joints, half a pint of whisky and flagrantly disrespecting the people who've so kindly come to support us.

[Once [D] has found someone he brings them up on stage, holding the mag up next to them as a comparison]

D: Y'alright my darling? Tell the baying mass your name *[he waits for her to do so]* that's quite the pretty name. And what's my name? *[He waits for her to give him a name. Same as before]*

Welcome to, who in the audience looks most like the front cover of our porn mag I'm [D] and I'll be your host for the next 30 seconds. At this point I'm averaging a 7 and a half with each show so let's try and improve on that –
Your girl on the cover over here is named Candy by the way, which I think we can all agree is a pretty shitty name for a sex symbol as it makes you think of children licking things.

So points out of ten, how much does *[her name]* look like our porn star?

[He begins to take bids as if an auctioneer on how close a resemblance he's found in his newest choice. Once a number has been decided on the music calms down and he addresses his selection one last time]

D: Thank you *[their name]* for your participation tonight in what I can only describe as ritualistic humiliation in front of your friends and or family. Objectifying women is something of a hobby of mine as you might have noticed and I'm glad you could be a part of that. Now mosey on down to rejoin the scum, after all, I only put you on a pedestal, they're the ones who judged you.

[Like a gentleman he lets her down before returning to the mic]

D: That's it, bask in my sexy accent and shit hair.

I sat with a homeless guy the other day,

I say the other day, we wrote this almost a year ago now so

I sat with this homeless guy a while off,

I say homeless

Offered some change to this poor bastard lying on a bench in the middle of the night in some park.

Told me to piss off, said he was just tired and wanted a lie down

So I get talking to your man on the bench, said his name was *[he gestures to a new audience member and encourages them to come up with a name for the not homeless guy, in the story this will be represented with a '_____']* right, said his name was _____ and we're chatting away and he's wearing this suit, got a bit of wine sort of stained down the middle but other than that he's actually looking quite swanky not homeless at all, and we share this bench together for a bit, he gives me the last dregs of his wine and I roll a joint to share which he can only take two puffs of before giving up like a massive fanny. He's genuinely pleasant, a nice guy, a student like me – psychology or psychotherapy, something to that effect and I managed to spend a good hour just on this bench chatting cartoons and music and the like before –

Before I sensed that real interesting connection. The one that really tickles the back of my brain, see, I have that nagging feeling in me that makes me feel special even though every human alive today has it, that tasty little fantasy that says 'I was born in the wrong fucking time me'. Doesn't matter when so much, maybe you wanted

to party it up in the Sixties with whoever it was invented
music before my generation came along and ruined it or
maybe you're more of a literary type, wanting to have
conversations with hemingway or shakespeare or some
other faggot that we learn to hate in school. Doesn't matter,
all these fantasies are is begging to have your shit life in a
place with more diseases, worse clothing and bigger idiots.
May as well holiday in the Middle East for all it means. Me
though, my shit life would make a marked amount more
sense if I had been born exactly a thousand years before I
was. I mean *[he marks out someone in his audience]* how old
do you think I am sir/m'am?
Be generous.

*[He takes whatever age he's given and attempts to figure when he
would have been born]*

[After a moment of confusion someone tosses him a calculator]

I'm a drummer I can only count to four

Right so you think I was born *[Whenever]* Minus 1000
years we're looking at the year *[Whatever]* the back end of
the Viking era. And, I'll give you that those crazy bastards
got a lot wrong, little too rape and pillage happy for the
auld conscience here not to perk up and start making those
annoyingly guilty noises it makes, but they got one thing
spot on.

They made kicking the shit out of each other for no reason
an integral part of the human experience.

And don't get me wrong, I like not bleeding as much as the
next man
but we've really not evolved too far from that caveman
mentality in my view.

Watch outside the *[nearest and scummiest club to the venue]* of
a friday night and you'll see those scrawny little pissweasals
spatting over who's trying to stick what in who and when.

That old caveman rage raises its barely pubescent looking head and bares its teeth.

Shouts of

B: *fuk yoo l-lkin at?*

E: *i'll have you! Notinthatwaythough-yabigfag.*

[a mic has slowly been lowered down from the ceiling, preferably by a member of the cast with a crude pulley system]

D: But all you're really hearing is –

[Loud, boxing style bell noise (cow bell on the drumkit perhaps.) and [D] takes the hanging mic, announcing the combatants as they size each other up in their douchebag fashion]

D: In the Red corner wHaying in at a measly 154 pounds, is a misplaced desire to fit in and seem like a big man twisted by too many jaeger bombs into the violent tantrums that old people use as an excuse to limit our freedoms as best they can.

And in the Blue corner wHaying in at 9000 pounds a year is the collective identity crisis of everyone born after the late Eighties and the dread inspired by our incredibly insecure future and the niggling suspicion that none of this is our fucking fault.

I like a good fight me.

[[B] and [E] box]

Is

  I suppose
    what I'm saying

And it seemed to me that your not so homeless man there did as well judging from the little scratches and grooves on his knuckles.

And that's fine bit of fucking fisticuffs now and then never hurt anybody far as I'm concerned.

That sounds, bad.

Well, in my view,

kicking the shit out of each other is like anal, it has to be two consenting adults and you'll find its a lot easier to get into it if you're both drunk.

But all jokes aside –

Shit.

     Ahhhhhhh
Shit.

[For a moment he scrambles around with the bits of script on stage, searching for his line. Perhaps the other actors improvise abuse or perhaps we're left in stony, awkward silence]

[[D] gives up]

Bet you feel real fucking awkward now don't you? Little bit of adrenaline pumping through your system wondering if the actor's forgotten his line or if this is another one of those obnoxious fucking tricks. *[a chuckle]* We named tonight 'ANGRY' and here and there you'll probably get elements of that, heh, the fact that 90% of this play should've been named 'Pondering' is our fault for all having fucking ADHD and his *[motioning to [C]]* for being a lazy writer. You you get how this works now don't, don't,

Don't giggle and look away just cause the actor's talking to you, you've seen like 20 minutes of this show I'm frankly insulted you haven't figured out that audience participation is the only thing keeping you lot entertained –

[[E] has won the boxing match]

E: ARE YOU NOT ENTERTAINED!

D: I wanna

Oi, I wanna ask you a question *[he looks to [C] briefly who seems oddly calm about [D]'s improv]* tonight was supposed to be about what makes us angry, but I don't think they really

know – you know? So I'm forced to reach out and bring
in a little bit more audience participation what makes you
angry? Not pissy, not urrrrgh and annoyed, what makes
you real fucking angry?

I'll tell you what gets me riled up
what gets me dark and dirty,

what SpeakS to the SpiderS living in my Soul and makeS
me loSe my Shit,

When I'm sitting on a bench in the middle of the night
intoxicatingly intoxicated and this
suit wearing
heavy drinking
cartoon watching
20 something year old
Crashing out on a park bench

Is someone I'm enjoying getting to know, another
bearskin-clad beserker amongst the skinny jeans and
frappalapacinno, sticking it to the man with one breath and
sticking it to your wife with the other.
No I don't know what I mean either.

I'm enjoying his company. That is until I venture to ask
the question of how he came to be under his very certain
circumstances.

and pretty quickly he loses it
starts slabbering the bag out of his girl there,
whining away,
teary eyed
like well, a massive fanny.

He says him and his girl there have just been at some
party, fancy catholic shit or something, a wedding, and
judging by the state of his face all stubble and grey eyes he
didn't really belong there. Especially if it was anything like
the kind of bullshit posh wedding my mum and dad used
to take me to.

And then, ha
Then, all the pieces started to click together.

Now maybe your man _____ really did like getting into
fights,

But trust my keen gaelic ears when I say I could hear the
guilt dripping from his voice like the last droplets of piss
that won't come off no matter how hard you shake.

And I remember,
I remember seeing the look he gave me when he noticed
that I'd noticed what I'd noticed
and I've seen that look before, nobody looks that guilty
over a fist fight with some douchebag at a party.

*[[B] who throughout these proceedings has been smoking what
looks to be a blunt, now returns to the mic and begins the next
song, the speech is interwoven with the lyrics, [E] and [A] rise as
the music begins to play]*

B: Blood is thicker than water.

D: Now I'd never met this girl of his, but I've seen my fair
share of scum like this guy, no matter how shitty your
other half gets no one should ever be in a position to make
that face.

B: Mother brother father sister son and daughter

D: And I'd be lying if I said there weren't times where I just
wanted to break someone's neck for things that weren't
their fault.

B: Action Hero fights foes face to fist

D: But it should not be possible to kick the shit out of
someone you care for

B: Family entertainment gets no better than this.

[The song drops and as it does [E] begins to viciously beat [A]]

B: Hello, My name is _____

I'm gonna tell you all a story bout what it is I've gone and done

I'm a good man, a good father and son

I pay my taxes, tip my waiters and I look down on none

But I spend eight hours a day shovelling shit in a sense

LoW Wage Work Where they spared all the expense

Although it's hard I like my life I do my best to get by

But we all have days where we lay down and die

I'm empty you see and all the love in the world

Can't fill the hole where the abuse is hurled

Maybe Dad wanted better or Mum expected worse

Could've been a huge lawyer or started snatching purses

[The hyper-violent scene on stage is interrupted as a young woman in the audience hurriedly leaves causing as much commotion as is possible whilst looking like she is attempting to cause as little commotion as possible – it is important that the audience see her face as she leaves. Without missing a beat in the song [E] and [C] share a nod and [E] dives into the audience and follows her out of the building looking worried, [A] slightly bemused by the whole affair and now lacking anything to do goes and sits down, sipping another drink]

Blood is thicker than water

Mother brother father sister son and daughter

Action hero fights foes face to fist

Family entertainment gets no better than this

The frustration of expectation to do well in this world

Shouting to the void with a voice thats never heard

Pushed me to do things only a monster could

Made loved ones feel fear like they never should

Scratch-knuckle-blood cause I refuse to choose

An option where not everyone has to lose

Because I grew up on T.V. I know there's no excuse

But when you're as angry as me it feels too good to let loose

I know that I mean it when I tell you I love you

That's why I leave you every night looking like somebody's mugged you

Blood is thicker than water

Mother brother father sister son and daughter

Action hero fights foes face to fist

Family entertainment gets no better than this

#4 Filling time before the phoned-in climax and Stand up-tragedy

[The song comes to a close and there is a pause, [E] has yet to return, [A], rather annoyed by this, turns to [D] and coaxes a beat out of his drums before returning to the mic]

A: Ladies and gentleman we interrupt tonight's showing of 'Angry' for more offensive but ultimately worthless content as we wait for the fifth actor to get his rear in gear and come back to the stage.

For your viewing pleasure we present, '12 things you can still be murdered for even though it's the 21st motherfucking century'

[the words of the next section can be taken up by the actors as they see fit, [C] will not join in. The atmosphere must be electric, they are building to a climax and they can see the cracks in the show starting to form, each of them finds each murder both hilarious

and infuriating and reads out the horrors as if it were Eurovision results.]

1.) Being raped – still a crime in the Middle East but don't look too smug Christians, not too long ago you guys were forcing rape victims to marry their rapists like the barbarians you are.

2.) Carrying Skittles in Florida and being black – have you all already forgotten? Shame on you, bullet to the heart and your obviously guilty assailant gets off scot free.

3.) Carrying out your duty as a doctor – abortion doctor George Tiller shot 5 times in the Nineties and finally murdered in the Noughties (fuck that word by the way) for saving women's lives. It's not okay to kill small clumps of cells living in a woman's uterus but it is okay to kill someone whose legal job it is to kill said cells. Great job America. Ya really got dem morals right didn't y'all.

4.) Defecting from Russia – poison in your tea.

5.) Not wanting Russia to invade your country – *[in a phony accent]* What is that Ukraine? I cannot hear your differing opinion over the sound of my tank crushing your citizens. Now excuse me while I ride shirtless through the barren wilderness on a fucking bear.

6.) Being gay in Russia. – Seriously. Fuck Russia.

7.) Crimes you didn't commit – according to smarter people than us, 4.1% of all American death row inmates didn't even do anything.

8.) Drawing cartoons – Muslims, I can do what I want you fucking crybabies. Calm down. There is no God.

9.) Being brown in a sandy country and near our soldiers. –Killing people is bad so we went to Iraq and killed all the people to stop them killing people. Which is of course, bad. Also oil.

10.) Being a good person – Chealsea Elizabeth Manning born Bradley Edward Manning leaked proof of every government in the goddamn world being a bunch of corrupt bastards and what happened? Solitary confinement for 35 years and nobody seemed to give a shit. Yeah it's not death but it might as well have been.

When you grow up son maybe you'll be a hero, and be severely punished for it by the corrupt and the stupid. And the older generation wonders aloud why us lot never seem to put any effort in or try to do well.

[[E] re-enters]

Ah good, you're back.

[The music dies.]

E: *[Taking the mic off of the stand, he approaches his speech like a stand-up comedian despite his speech being unfunny. He is more self deprecating and nervous than charming as if he's not used to performing]* You ever wonder if people got in your head they'd be impressed at how hard your life is –

I

I'm not saying my life is hard

Or that yours aren't – although you look like you haven't had much to do with your time. Not too many shoulders to cry on if you know what I mean

No I'm not saying my life is hard in fact I'm saying the opposite,

To me everything I have to deal with is relatively simple, but do you ever wonder if maybe you're just fucking brilliant at dealing with problems and if like you could swap brains with someone they'd be like 'ah shiiit nigaah'!

Oh that word offends you? It's not okay but shit, cunt, shitcunt, fuck, faggot, fanny pussyhole silly bitch retard "Dying of AIDS in an ironic 'Thought they'd die of hunger' way" whore-killer PigFucker, Christians are rape supporting mentalists with no bullshit detection that shit's fine for you is it?

Titwank. *[beat]* Dirty, diseased cock sucking whores who when they aren't turning tricks, fisting cunts and pumping dicks for spare change they're locked in my basement writing most of my material.

Sorry I,

Get a bit carried away

Seriously though I did make sure they put 'not for the faint of heart' on the poster I'm a try squeeze a 9/11 joke in at the end of this speech and everything just so you know.

Where the fuck was I?

C: twenty/six

E: /Coolio.

Yeah

Yeah. Am I the only one with this question? No one else wonders about what strangers'd feel like in your body? It used to be the only thing I was scared of

As a kid I mean.

Waking up in a situation where I had no concept of the skills required to finish it like maybe I'd switch brains with a surgeon or something, midway through a tracheotomy which involves making an incision in the neck to allow the patient to breathe, either permanently or temporarily and is fucking tricky as balls mate.

Maybe that's why I tended to absorb facts, in case I ever needed them.

[He indicates a section of his neck] Tracheotomy incision'd go there if you were wondering.

In case your mum can't breathe and all you have to hand is a scalpel and a taste for adventure.

I suppose if I told you I was the somewhat neurotic one it wouldn't really help you set me apart from this lot.

I'm the comedian, I'm kinda funny, I'm kinda hard to follow a little bit maybe perhaps and if you're not paying too much attention I'll just keep extending this sentence until you start to pick up on that fact and it becomes funny to you and regardless of your sense of humour you could at least be impressed at how this sentence is grammatically correct, no green wavy lines on WORD or anything are you with me yet okay good.

My speech is quiet and short I'll barely have time to stand up before the comedy is done.

I have had sex with 6 women. I have never got less than a B in an exam

My mother loves me
My father is proud of me
Sometimes I drink with friends
I have a girlfriend who makes me happy
Maybe I will marry her

My life is quiet and short

The title of my autobiography will be

'Stand-up Tragedy, how my life went swimmingly so I killed myself'.

[He turns to sit down before quickly spinning back to the mic]

Oh yeah, What's the difference between a cow and 9/11?

Americans can't milk a cow for 14 years.

And I can't milk a scene for more than 2 minutes.

So

     Bye

Bye

Bye buh bye bye byeee bbeeeey bye.

I'm bad at endings

[he trails off]

[He turns to [C] looking a little bit helpless]

Did you wanna...? You know I'm kind of, I think I'm losing them a bit.

[[C] looks at [E] expressionlessly before handing him a few sheets of script and a small knife. [E] perks up a bit and has a quick look at what he's been given before looking nervous again]

E: Oh

I thought we...

You're sure?

[[C] isn't even looking at him anymore]

[[E] takes a deep breath and visibly changes from nervy to posturing and aggressive, he is reading [C]'s lines for him]

E: You know me, I'm the one you wish you were, I'm the one that does all the things you wished you'd done.

Remember that prrrrick, at that club you love to go to, who squeezed your girlfriend's arse as he walked past? I'm the one who kicks him in the head and stamps on his nads. I'm the one with goolies enough to get kicked out of that club. I'm the one who goes to those parties you always felt uncomfortable at, snorts a load of that ever-so enticing powder you wish you'd tried just once and ended up makking off with whoever it is (guy or girl makes no odds to me) that you told yourself "One day I'll profess my undying love to them."

And I'm the one with the ego big enough to get up on a stage and tell you just how fucking brilliant I think I am.

[Speeding up]

The one who can talk to stangers without feeling a sense of dread. Me.

The one who dumps someone without breaking their heart.

The one who doesn't immediately get back with them and feel like a giant pussy for it.

The one who picked up smoking young enough for it to still look cool.

The one who tells their boss to fuck off when they're being a proper bastard.

The one who can handle his drink.

[Picking up on a man in the audience]

E: What's your name pal?

[No matter the man's response:]

E: Nah that's shit. *[To a woman]* What's your name gorgeous? *[No matter her response:]* Lovely, that's my name that.

A: What you doing you prick?

E: The fuck you say to me?

A: *[hushed]* We worked hard at this, there's a fucking structure.

E: Piss off

D: Alright calm your shit

B: This again.

E: Just QUIET, let me work this at my own pace,

B: Not if you keep fucking us around like

A: Just chill

B: I fucking knew this'd happen

E: Just let me do THIS

D: eh.

A: Guys

E: Mate

D: People are watching

A: Guys

D: Gents

B: Can you do this properly?

E: Mate I will fucking hurt you –

D: Get your shit together lads

E: if you keep carrying on

B: Piss off, you're half my size.

[[E] whips out the switchblade and embeds it in the table]

E: Don't think I'm some sort of fucking pussy!

[The ensuing silence makes him out to be just that]

[[A] looks less than shocked]

[[B] stares at the knife as if thinking of the next silly thing to do]

[[C] hasn't stirred from his position in the slightest]

[[D] has instinctively risen out of his seat as if to defend the others]

[[E] regains a modicum of composure and returns to the mic]

E: I'm the one

I'm the one you knew of in school. I'm the one who failed
harder than you at your GCSE's, I'm the one who tortured
seagulls on the playing field. I'm the one that had more
fun, fucks, fights, fireworks and friends
than you did
        as a kid.

I'm the one who has a baby before they're even close to being ready. I'm the one who sees six months of the inside of a minimum security prison for minor offenses – let out after four for good behaviour and being a little bitch. I'm that old friend you see walking round your old home town looking old and tired when you've just bought your first home and got engaged to a pretty – but not too pretty so you know she's stable – woman and all you're able to do when you look at me is look at something else.

I'm the one who never had a mum,
or never had a dad
or had too little of either
or too much of both
So when you see me sitting small working in some sorry corner shop you pretend,
You don't remember me, but I remember you, every one of you
'cause I was so very steady and sure of foot and ready to be amazing in the days where I knew the likes of you,
When I didn't know, that I had to know
The purpose of having a purpose
How hard you have to work just to survive in the first world
How loud you have to scream to have your voice heard in a country run by types who don't have to steal to eat but steal anyway and I just don't understand WHY.

You think I wanna be an actor? A rapper or a fucking rockstar? You think I wouldn't rather lead revolutions by writing slow rhyming poetry and sitting down to wait for it to happen? You think I want to go to university to prove to the world that I know how to write an essay and sign my name on the dotted line?

Of course I don't
But nobody listens to a pre-school teacher.

[he pauses, allowing a moment before returning to his previous character]

E: Uhh yeah?

B: Siq mate.

A: For a minute I almost thought he wasn't a prick

For a minute

[The joke falls flat as [C] ignores them, he is, after all, a prick]

#5 George Osborne is an oxygen thief

*[[F] approaches for her speech, she's sweet, quieter than the rest
and although she's barely spoken up to this point she has as much
nuts as the rest of the cast]*

F: So I'm kinda shy, you might've *[beat]* you've noticed.
Some people say that the shy ones are the scariest. Which
is Fucking silly. I'm safe, you don't have to

Worry
I'm not like her *[[A]]* at all. But I like to think I'm pretty
[she approaches someone in the audience, a man] do you think
I'm pretty mister? *[She waits for a response, it should be as
horrible a wait as possible]* What a lovely thing for you to say
under pressure
[gaining a little confidence] don't worry mister I'm not like,
coming on to you. I'm not so into the cock. You know
how it is, for a play to be good, there's gotta be at least AN
lesbian. It's art innit. So you're safe *[turning to a woman in
the audience]* You however I could stare at all night, what's
your name beautiful? *[waits for a response]* Huh that's my –
mother's name, how Freudian.

She's dead

Oh that's funny is it I'm sorry, I thought we were
performing to human beings not the soulless orc armies of
the mighty lord sauron

*[Throughout this speech she has been checking her watch at
appropriate moments, she does again now and catches herself
doing it]* Sorry, I'm not bored I promise, its just. Ah

Well

[checks watch] We have time for more bullshit don't we.

Okay, ah, well, I'm one of those paranoid types, as in – can't cross the road without looking both right, left, then right again because a car could definitely have started speeding towards me in the time it took for me to move my head right then left then right again. I'm also incredibly accident prone.

[she motions to her feet] don't know if you can see from down there

very small feet

fall over a lot

yeah.

And well, I don't know about you dashingly confident types but I'm immensely scared of dying.

So *[checks watch]* a year and 7 months ago I did something real stupid

I sat down and worked out when I'd die

I mean like in a vague way

I'm not Jesus

But I figured what, at the rate I smoke don't eat healthy and basically drip feed myself *[Actress's favourite form of alcohol, don't pretend she doesn't have one]* I figure I won't live much longer than 70, which a year and 7 months ago gave me 50 years left give or take.

Half a million minutes in a year
25 million minutes left to live
I've spent *[however many minutes the show runs x the number of runs this cast has done]* of those just running this play.

Kinda makes you real anxious I'm afraid.

Every second slipping by laughing at you cause you couldn't make it mean something.

Little bit terrifying

[pause]

Oh god I'm so sorry I don't mean to be such a downer *[she giggles, but not in a way that makes the situation better]*

You know they told us to improvise as much of this as we like but I don't think I'm very good at judging a room...

Uh

Anyway this is a song about dead people

[The band launches into a softer song]

[Note: the lyrics of this song should grow and change with the times, eg. When it's been too long since Leonard Nimoy's death replace him with your favourite recently dead celebrity]

SONG #2 Why is everyone I hate still alive?

Why is Philip Seymour Hoffman Dead?
Or that guy from The Sopranos?
Why was Cobain shot in the head?
These are things that we all know.

But the question bothering me
Is why do I never see
In the papers or on TV
That George Osborne tried to waterski
And drowned in the fucking sea

Why is everyone I hate still alive? (Still alive)
Why is everyone I hate STILL alive? (STILL alive)
He's been a thorn in my side   (the cunt)
Since two thousand and fucking five (what a cunt)
Why is George Osborne still alive? (Still alive)

Why did Leonard Nimoy have to die?
No it's not too soon grow the fuck up.
And why did the doctor have to lie,
When he said grandma could get her hopes up?

But the real question bothering me
Is why do I never see
In the papers or on TV
That while out drinking afternoon tea
Farage was crushed by falling debris

Why is everyone I hate still alive? (Still alive)
Why is everyone I hate STILL alive? (STILL alive)
I want the bastard to die   (The cunt)
'cause my girlfriend's not EU certified (ooh foreign)
O Why is Nigel Farage still alive? (Still alive)

How can anyone believe in karma
When serial killers like Jeffrey Dahmer
Murdered innocent fuckers with scorn
But allowed the Kardashians to be born

But the question bothering me
Is why do I never see
In the papers or on TV
That whoever commissioned TOWIE
Has been stung by a killer bee

Why is everyone I hate still alive? (Still alive)
Why is everyone I hate STILL alive? (STILL alive)
I hope they all get stabbed in the eye
With no possibility of revival
Why is everyone I hate still alive? (Why is everyone I hate
still alive?)

Why is everyone I hate still alive?
Why is everyone I hate still alive
It's great that Thatcher's burning in Hell
But she might've taken her party with her as well
O Why is everyone I hate still alive
Still alive?

#6 The creamy climax all up inside ya

A: *[Calmly]* Hows it going muthafuckaaaas? You drunk yet?
We've been working under
and been perfectly happy with
the assumption that nobody likes this play when they're
sober so...

if you're not drunk,

I hope you're pretty fuckin' high...

But

If you're over twenty-nine
or you have "work in the morning" we have this little
section for you

For the minority of you that came in here with

innocence in your souls

and hopes in your hearts

Of finding a fucking work of art

tucked away in the middle of nowhere

For the few

who

walked in wanting to not be offended by

everything they see

This is for those of you, who haven't heard

how hard we've worked to make you happy

and to prove to you we have a place in the world

you who tell us to tone down

the tittyfucking tourrettes syndrome fuck you slowly scenes

For those who haven't got the fucking balls to see

that when we say 'Some people need

to be

insulted'

We mean you

this scene is for you

just for you

all for fuckin' you

this is the safe scene even your granny could see.

This is my story and fuck me is it ever so innoffensive

A: *[Narrating herself]* She lights a cigarette *[she does so]* exhales *[she does so]* and she begins *[she does so]*.

I was born and raised by people who're hollow on the inside. But you knew that. The swiftest route to
an attitude like this
an outfit like this
and hips that do this *[she wiggles]*

Is parents so scared of living you're surprised they had the where withal to become parents in the first place.

And from there you can start to piece the story together yourselves. You're not stupid and I'm not subtle, the kid with nothing to live for wallowing in so much cliché that it's frankly impressive anyone has the gall to moan about it in this day and age.

So mum and dad pissed up their
shitty little,
squitty little
lives, trading in personalities for first kiddies and then

A+E: THE ALMIGHTY HAND OF GURD

A: Which is of course how I ended up being dragged door to door every Sunday afternoon ruining people's days by making them feel awkward over shit they didn't care about.

Smart motherfuckers in the audience starting to twig now are you? Little pieces of the proverbial puzzle slotting together? Well that's the idea kiddies.

So I'm stood on the doorstep of this jittery looking kid. Basically breathing smoke for how fucking high he was. And I start to feel those,
feelings.

Stirrings.

Ladies you know what I'm talking about, guys maybe less so. That *[she begins to grind]* fluttery throb

Longing

but in such as way as to feel whole at the same time.

And this dude's not much to look at but the way he so clearly wants me, not giving a fuck about what my dad thought – it was, invigorating. So he's rude to the paper thin strawman of a catholic chaplain guy thing who goes storming off with a sort of

E: Hw urg? BLURGH Shnur glerp BRRAAARG!

A: And I'm left trying to figure out what it is I'm feeling towards this guy.

The sex was great

At least that's what I told him, but I'm pretty sure I meant it.

When we did it for the first time – ah fuck – we just lay there for hours after and I shook, just shook, my body wouldn't work for me it was fucking incredible.

So we'd do that

A lot.

We used to just lie in bed watching telly, he seemed so excited by it, it was cute, I remember *[she giggles]* we used to skip school just to watch the teleshopping and music channels and all that shit that normal people don't watch.

I really did love that fucking idiot.

Until

[She refers to [C] by the name given to the not homeless man in [D]'s story]

'til,

uh, [C] I'm not too
          I'm not comfortable
          I don't wanna
              do this bit. Not on...

[half-heartedly] Please. I don't want it to be about that anymore.

[Pause. Too long of a one]

C: Then do something better.

[pause]

A: But isn't this the,

point?

[All eyes on [C].]

[[C] shrugs]

A: Fine, *[She mentally skips ahead in her speech]* I stopped seeing him after my sister's wedding.

Left home.
Tried to get a job.
Failed to get a job.

Went to university,
dropped out of university.

Got pregnant,
had the kid

[pause, she is trying to provoke her audience now]

Kid died. Smoked a marijuana cigarette so now I'm into crack
Whored myself on the streets to pay for my addiction, felate you fifty times a day for a fiver?

Killed my dad and fucked my mum

.

Got crucified for made-up reasons

.

See it doesn't matter does it, the stories are meaningless nobody gives the slightest shit do they?

[The next few lines should be a description of how the actress actually got to the point of performing this show, below is an example-written for the 2015 NSDF performance of ANGRY in Scarborough]

You wanna know how I actually got here? I worked my fucking arse off, paid attention in school, bluffed my way into higher education, met him and him, followed by him, him, her and her then all of us slaved ourselves half to death to raise the exploitatively high amount of money it costs to stand on this spot and perform to you specific set of people. Jumped in a van with someone we didn't know and crammed ourselves into the student halls of Scarborough campus.

Don't fucking matter though, Does it? Nothing changes when you know our stories.

Don't fucking matter.

You know who I am? I'm [A] and I wanna be more than a fucking young person statistic, I wanna be in a play that makes you think AND do something, I wanna be someone who inspires everyone who sees me standing here as exposed as I am
to be better

[As she speaks [B] and [D] have risen and approached their own mics and begin to perform the final Poem/Song: Angry, maybe there is music now, certainly there is later]

B: Look at me

D: Who am I to you?

A: I want all the things that
scare me so much that
every inch of me is fucking paralysed

B: Am I interesting yet?

A: To be a cautionary tale
for future motherfuckers to learn from

D: Have I proved myself to you yet?

A: Drink, smoke, fuck as much as you like
It's cunting brilliant

B: Do you love me?

D: Could you beat me?

B: Do you need me?

B/D: Yet?

A: And I will will do my very fucking best to build a better place for you to do that in.

B: Would you be happy
   If the last sight you see
   Was me
   With my hands wrapped round your throat
   Choking
   The last of a life well spent
   From the inside of your neck

A: But if you're my kid
   in ten years watching this on video
   and for some reason you believe me,
   know that I'm trying

B: Or you reckon
   you could take me in a fair fight?

D: Bit o' fuckin'

B: Fisticuffs

D: Never hurt anyone

B: Far as we're concerned

A: We are trying our best, *[She checks her watch, we realise it was [F]'s before,]* but our time is only worth 6.50 an hour

   [[E] has joined the poem]

E: People paid hard earned pounds

D: To purchase tickets

E: Money meant to be

D: Spent to be

E: Making life easier

A: *[[B] has handed her his joint]* And we're running out of it.
And in between fist fights to help forget ourselves, drugs
[she takes a drag] to drown out the pain, and T.V. to tell us
it's all gonna be okay
we gotta work all day to pay the rent.

[Beat]

So if the cycle repeats itself I'm sorry,
so much so I'll say
That it is our fault.

[The whole cast is ready]

But today we aren't to blame

C: Today

A/B/C/D/E/F: We are entertainment

THE CAST[ANY AND ALL]: We want you to know

It's okay to like us
Today
It's okay
to be
Just
Like us

Drowning in disappointment

Don't be better if
you don't want to
Just be happy with nothing happening

Forget us if your future isn't frightening
don't do drugs and don't start fighting

Just don't be surprised when we here all do
Tattooed up to the nines, carving questions into
Our wrists

Balling fists
'til the bossman says home time
We will scrape out of our alone time
a sense of senseless personalties
taught to believe that being 'me'
is enough to see
it
all for what
it
is.

We will not be blind to the risks
You took on our behalf
half-arsed as they may have been

But we are fuck ups
drugged up to the nuts
To cover up the fact
That we are the experiment
Generation
offered no real explanation
For our degeneration
and Forced into occupations
You had to create for us

I know the square route of 45
                              I know what year Hitler died
I dunno where I'll be in six months

On my gravestone it will say
that we played the *[name of the theatre you're in]* today
and nothing much changed thereafter

We are aimless
So we stole your names to be someone for a day
and when this song stops
so do we
and we're okay with that.

We are Angry.

And we hope you are too

We are messy
Messy in a 'you should do your best to forget me'
Sortof way

And we Know you are too

Even if it's just for one night only

C: There's ANGRY. This play is the political manifesto of a
    fucking mentalist. This play was a mess.
    You see even now we've no idea how to say what we
    struggle with.
    The insides of our heads are set with silly string and dicks,
    That brain melting headache you get after being alive too
    long.
    'Drinking-through-hangover-thinking' we call it.
    And who takes the blame in all this?
    Whose fault is it that it hurts to be awake most days?
    That I can't think straight even when I'm doing the one
    thing I love?
    She told you before, this play is called ANGRY and the
    last word of this play is me.

    But nowadays, nowadays I'm not so sure about that.

    [pause]

C: Thankyou.

    [The music crescendos and fades to a close]

    [It takes as long as it wants.]

    END

www.ingramcontent.com/pod-product-compliance
Ingram Content Group UK Ltd.
Pitfield, Milton Keynes, MK11 3LW, UK
UKHW031250020325
455689UK00008B/114